MY MAGNOLIA MEMORIES
(and Musings) In Poems

This book is dedicated to

My most loving, devoted husband,
Rufus James Dorsey Jr.
Thank you for always accepting
me just as I am, and always
encouraging me to 'do the right thing.'
and to
My son,
James Henry Dorsey,
who is the great love of my life .

My Magnolia Memories

(and Musings)
In Poems

— ◆ —

by
Patricia Neely-Dorsey

— ◆ —

GrantHouse Publishers
2012

ISBN: 978-1-935316-473

Copies of this book are available from:

Patricia Neely-Dorsey
1196 CR 681
Saltillo, MS 38866
(901) 848-6800
Email: magnoliagirl21@yahoo.com
WEB: www.patricianeelydorsey.webs.com

Published by GrantHouse Publishers
2101 Green Leaf Drive
Jonesboro, AR 72401
TEL: 901-218-3135
E-mail: granthousepub@aol.com

Cover design by Rainey Scott

Printed in the United States of America

TABLE OF CONTENTS

Dedication ii
Foreword.. ix
Southern Life x

SOUTHERN SIGHTS, SCENES and SENTIMENTS

Mississippi 1
(Steel) Magnolia 2
Natchez Trace 3
The Delta... 4
Memphis 5
Them Blues 6
A King of Swing 7
Back Roads 8
Made in Mississippi 8
Bottle Tree 9
Front Porch (Hospitality Headquarters) 10
Talkin' (Country) Southern 11
Southern Comfort (Food) 12
You Ain't Country 13
Spices (of Life) 14
Nicknames 14
Southerners Remember.. 15
Sweet Treats 15
The Truck Patch (Gone But Not)..................................... 16
(Various) Superstitions 17

SEASONS

Taste of Spring 18
Summer Sun.. 19

Summer Night Air 19
Highway Ride (In the Summertime) 20
Fall (In the Country) 21
Dawn by the Lake (Fall) 22

OLD TIMES

Old Tyme Christmas 23
The Shack 24
Back Porch Washer 25
(Un) Modern (In) Convenience 26

CHURCH

Old Time Religion 27
Saturday Night Ritual 28
Preacher's Wife (50's Style) 29
Fellowship Sunday 30
Visitation 31
Hat Lady 32

THE (Neighbor) HOOD – Back in the Day

Back In the day 33
Ole Skool 33
Miss Northside 34
Debros 36
AM Strange Library 37
Beauty Shop 38
The Pool Hall 39
The Club 40
Landmarks 41
Banks 42
Neighborhood Gossip (Minding Other Folks Business) 43

CHILDHOOD MEMORIES

Soul Train 44
Double Dutch 45
Spades 46
Cake Walk 47
Going to town 48
My Childhood Room 49
Getting In Trouble (What Our Parents Would Always Say) 50
4th of July 51
Making (Homemade) Icecream 52
Understood 52
Debutante Coutillion 53
The Hoodoo Lady 54

TUPELO

The Tupelo Spirit 55
Tupelo 56
The Birthplace 58
The King 59
Reed's Department Store 60

LOVE

Kudzu Love 61
Perfect 62
Home 63
Tell Me Again 64
Everything 65
Together (Again) 66
The Softer Side of Life 67
My Favorite Restaurant 68
The Eyes Have It 69
The Truck 70

It.. 70
Aberration 71
The Game of Love 72
Child's Play? 73

LOSS

Not Cinderella.. 74
Burned 75
Heartbreak 75
Questions 76
Seasons of Love 77
Invisible 78
Love Hurts 79
Disconnect.. 80

COMMENTS AND COMMENTARY

Who I Be? 81
Flavor 82
My Poems 83
Enough 83
Sistah Friends 84
My People 86
We Like to Read, Too 87
Family Tree 88
One 90

INSPIRATION/CONSOLATION

Consolation 93
Fearless 95
The Rock of Ages 96
Wondering 97
If Mississippi's In You.. 98

Foreword

During my many speaking engagements, I have always introduced my first volume of poems, <u>Reflections of a Mississippi-A Life In Poems</u>, as "celebration of the south and things southern."

One reviewer called <u>Reflections</u>, A "love letter to the South." Now, in <u>My Magnolia Memories and Musings</u>, the love affair continues.

There are so many negative connotations associated with Mississippi and the south in general, though in my poems, I attempt to give an upclose, personal and positive glimpse into the southern way of life.

I hope to dispel some of the many misconceptions and misunderstanding about our much maligned state and region. Though it might seem impossible to many people, there is MUCH to love about this place that I so fondly call home.

Enjoy the poems.

Patricia Neely-Dorsey

SOUTHERN LIFE

If you want a glimpse of Southern life,
Come close and walk with me;
I'll tell you all the simple things,
That you are sure to see.
You'll see mockingbirds and bumblebees,
Magnolia blossoms and dogwood trees,
Caterpillars on the step,
Wooden porches cleanly swept;
Watermelons on the vine,
Strong majestic Georgia pines;
Rocking chairs and front yard swings,
June bugs flying on a string;
Turnip greens and hot cornbread,
Coleslaw and barbecue;
Fried okra, fried corn, fried green tomatoes,
Fried pies and pickles, too.
There's ice cold tea that's syrupy sweet,
And cool, green grass beneath your feet;
Catfish nipping in the lake,
And fresh young boys on the make.
You'll see all these things
And much, much more,
In a way of life, that I adore.

--from Reflections of a Mississippi Magnolia-
A Life in Poems
Copyright 2008 Patricia Neely-Dorsey

MISSISSIPPI

In the heart of Dixie,
Perfumed by
The sweet, fragrant smell of magnolias
and serenaded with
The melodious songs of the mockingbird,
Lies a true Queen of the South.
Her name is Mississippi .
I don't know how to explain this place,
Except to say that she "speaks" to me.
The rocks, the flowers, the birds and trees
Speak to me.
They sometimes whisper,
And sometimes they shout;
But always they say,
"This is where you belong."

(STEEL) MAGNOLIA

Breathtaking,
Delicate beauty
Of Creamy Perfection
With Roots Running Deep
In Southern Soil,
A history almost
As old as time,
And endurance
As tough as
Steel;
She defies description
And explanation
But...
Beauty is its own excuse.

NATCHEZ TRACE

Indian foot trails
Turned busy pathways
For industrious merchants
And weary travelers
Burial mounds,
Battle fields,
Interesting artifacts
And
Amazing wildlife
At every turn
Scenic route
From Natchez to Nashville
History in my backyard

THE DELTA (Black, White and Blues)

**Flatlands stretching endlessly
Toward the horizen
As far as the eye can see;
Rich, black soil
Yields endless rows
Of blinding white wonder
On fertile ground
That gives birth to the blues.**

MEMPHIS

Hustling, Bustling City on the Bluff,
With music flowing through the streets
And soulful rhthyms floating in the air;
Known for B.B.'s Blues,
Elvis' Graceland,
And World Famous Barbecue
On the Mighty Mississippi;
You are Spirited, Vibrant, Intoxicating,
Southern to the bone
And... Unforgettable.

5

THEM BLUES

Somebody's always singing
Them Monday Morning blues songs
Them sho' nuff done me wrong songs
Them stayed out all night long songs
Them moaning, groaning love songs
Them bear your heart and soul songs
Them feel it in your bones songs
Them make you weak and strong songs
Them letting go and holding on songs
Them totally yours and mine songs
Them everybody knows songs...
We ALL love them blues...songs

A KING OF SWING (James Melvin Lunceford)
(born: June 6, 1902, Itawamba County, MS)

It's all the new thing,
They said of that swing;
It was a whole lot of jazz,
With an added pizzaz.
A Count and a Duke
Made the big bands sing;
But from the Southland,
There came a new king -
James Melvin Lunceford
Entered onto the world stage
And his bold, lively rhythms
Became all the rage.
With grand spectacle, showmanship, humor
And a flashy, unique style
He led his ensembles,
With a dazzling smile.
Born in a Mississippi hill town,
And ascending to great fame;
His renowned Lunceford two-beat,
Would, forever, cement his name.

(Orginally written for Lunceford Mississippi Blues Trail
Marker Dedication, in Fulton, MS.)

BACKROADS

Rocky,
Dusty,
Bumpy,
Curving,
Twisting,
Turning
Tree-Canopied pathways;
The Short cut
The Scenic Route
Or the long way home.

MADE IN MISSISSIPPI

Along with...
Syrupy, sweet, hospitality,
Downhome, Delta blues,
And beautiful Magnolia girls;
Strong family values,
Unbreakable bonds ,
And lifelong memories
Are Made in Mississippi.

BOTTLE TREE

They say
That evil spirits
Are captivated by your beauty
As you stand glistening in the sun.
Wanting a better look,
They come closer
And get caught.
That's what
They say.

FRONT PORCH
(Hospitality Headquarters)

Just the spot
For taking in a cool breeze
And watching the world go by
Friends and neighbors out
For a leisurely stroll
Stop and sit a spell.
"Lemonade"?
"Iced Tea"?
"Co-Cola?"
"Did you hear about...?"
"Do Tell!"
"You Don't Say!"
"My, how the time flies"
"Y'all come back, now"
"You here? "

TALKIN' (Country) SOUTHERN

Well I'll be!
Lawd a mercy!
How y'all doing?
We ain't seent y'all in a month of Sundays
Won't y'all sit a spell?
We was jus' fixin' to go to the store...
To make groceries
But it look like it's coming up a cloud
I reckon we best wait til that blow over
That last storm pert near blew us clean away
Our mailbox ended up way over yonder in
That pasture.
Who that you got wit' y'all?
Oh that's Johnny's boy!
He know he the spittin' imagine of that man!
He sho done growed.
He kinda favor his cousin, Joe, too.
That Joe ain't got a lick of sense.
Bless His Heart.
That whole family used to live right up
That road a piece
We know all his people.

SOUTHERN COMFORT (Food)

It's been announced about our state,
That we are the fattest in the nation;
We always top the "unhealthy list,"
It's always seems our station.
It's absolutely clear to me,
That the world would know just why;
If they'd ever been to South Pontotoc Grocery,
And tried the Peach Fried Pie.
The food in our state's so good,
There's just no parallel;
If eating good cooking were against the law,
We'd all certainly go to jail.
We've got some men who cook for us,
Like no woman ever could;
And passing up a plate of hot catfish,
Now, tell me one who would.
Yes, everything is filled with fat,
Or fried deeply in some grease;
And if our tea's not sweet enough,
We can hardly keep our peace.
We all want to "live our best life,"
Be healthy and all of that;
But, unfortunately in our fair state,
It's SO delicious getting fat.

YOU AIN'T COUNTRY

If you've never...
Swept the front yard (No, not the porch but the yard),
Played under the porch (Yes, under)
Intentionally eaten dirt
(Not just any dirt, mind you, that good ole
red clay kind)
Gone barefoot outside...all day
And seen old car tires used as
Flower planters and yard decorations and swings...
You ain't country.
If you've never...
"Sopped" syrup or gravy with a biscuit
Shelled the peas for your supper or
Drank coffee from the saucer
You ain't country
If you don't know what a truck patch is
Or about the grease can on top of the stove
Or that canning vegetables does NOT involve a can...
You ain't country.
If you've never used a mason jar as a drinking glass
Or to eat milk and bread from
Or to catch fireflies in..
Or to cut out homemade biscuits with...
You ain't country.
And, if you're not shaking your head in agreement
And smiling a bit as you remember....
I know for sure
You ain't country!

THE SPICE(S) OF LIFE

Sugar on Peas
Sugar on Grits
Sugar in Tea
And hotsauce
On EVERYTHING

NICKNAMES

"What's his name?"
"Who?...
Pee Wee,
Peanut,
June Bug,
Dimp, Shine,
Bird, Snake, Rat,
Shortie, Buddy,
Mack?"
"Yeah...
But what's his "real name?"
"Beats me..."
"We just always call him
That."

SOUTHERNERS REMEMBER
(We remember when)

Southern folks remember when
All of the stores in town
(except maybe a few gas stations)
Closed on Sundays...
Everyone went to church
And the preacher was always invited
To someone's house to eat after services.
We remember when
Cars pulled off to the side of the road
As a funeral procession passed...
And when the whole "village"
Really DID help raise the child.

❖ ❖ ❖

SWEET TREATS

Banana Pudding
Peach Cobbler
Tea cakes
Mississippi Mud Pies
Chocolate Gravy
And fresh Ambrosia
Are "sweet as can be"
And "simply southern" treats.

15

THE TRUCK PATCH (Gone...But Not)

I pass a familiar spot
As I go on my way
A place now desolate
And laid bare
By bulldozers and heavy machinery
Eating away at the landscape
Day by day
Each day I note the changes to a place
Still laden with childhood memories
A place now gone...but not
Once, this was "The Truck Patch"
A thriving community garden
Of lush, green, growing things
Where neighbors planted together
And harvested together
Thankful for the offerings brought forth
From the red clay earth.
It was a place where children laughed and played
Played and picked...but mostly played
The adults laughed and talked
Talked and worked
But mostly worked
It was a place of sharing and love
It's a place now gone...but not
Because, I will never forget.

(Various) Superstitions

I must admit we Southerners
Are a superstitious lot
And some can be quite serious
About the beliefs we've got.
"Don't walk beneath a ladder,"
"Don't step on a sidewalk crack;"
"You're best to go around it,
Or you'll break your mother's back;"
"Don't let a black cat cross your path,"
Or let a broom sweep across your feet;
Don't ever break a mirrored glass,
Or bad luck you're sure to meet."
The old folks would say
"Remember these things,
And hold on to them fast;
If you neglect any one of them,
Your good times sure won't last."

A TASTE OF SPRING

Birds singing
Grass greening
Colors blinging
Nature's springing

(Southern) SUMMER SUN

Streaming Rays of Beaming Light
Gleaming Rays of Dazzling Bright
Is the Southern, Summer Sun

◆ ❖ ◆

(Summer) NIGHT AIR

The Summer night air
Envelops like a blanket
Thick,
Heavy,
Comforting
And completely still.

HIGHWAY RIDE (In the Summertime)

**Clear, blue sky
Above expanses of green
Divided by strips of gray
Surrounded by sprinkles of
Yellow, pinks, purples and white
Highway ride in the summertime.**

* It is often joked that the four seasons in Mississippi are: Almost Summer, Summer, Still Summer and Christmas.

FALL (In The Country)

Floating slowly to the ground
Like delicate snowflakes
And crunching underfoot with each
movement
Autumn leaves blanket the ground
In dazzling shades
Of Red, Yellow, Orange and Gold
A deer darts through the woods
As hunters await.

DAWN (By The Lake)

Magnificent ribbons of orange
Streak the morning sky
As speckles of light dance on still, calm leaves
Illuminating each vein.
A dreamlike mist hovers
Above the quiet waters
Disappearing, as the world awakes.

OLD TYME CHRISTMAS

A live tree from the woods
With Popcorn trim
And Candy canes;
Apples, Oranges,
Peppermints,
And some nuts;
A doll,
A ball,
A truck
And a pair of skates
To share.

THE
SHACK

Plain,
Dull,
Drab,
No Paint,
Tin Roof,
Facilities
Outside
But
Home.

BACK PORCH WASHER

**Round tub
On Legs
And sometimes rollers
Ready for those
Monday "washday "blues
Putter, Putter
Swish, Swish
Shake Shake
Water spitting everywhere;
Clothes finally clean
And tub drained dry
Now, feed them through the wringers
And watch your fingers
Please!**

(Un) MODERN (In)CONVENIENCE

Winter Time.
Late Night.
Gotta Go!
Outhouse?
Too Cold.
Too Far.
Nightpot.

OLD TIME RELIGION

Long,Wooden Benches
Creaky wood floors
The only air Conditioning...
An open window and
And funeral home fans
Raise your finger and tip out quietly
To be excused.
Giving honor to God....
Welcome, Welcome, Welcome
Whosonever will..let him come.
The doors of the church are open

SATURDAY NIGHT RITUAL
(Back in the day)

Y'all children come in now."
"It's time to get ready."
Clothes laid out
And Sunday School lessons to learn
Water heated on the stove,
And baths for everyone
In the big tin tub.
From the youngest to the oldest
Or the oldest to the youngest,
Everyone gets a turn.
Because...
"Cleanliness is next to godliness."
And after all...
Tomorrow is "The Lord's Day."

PREACHER'S WIFE (50's Style)

Tall,
Regal,
Sophisticated,
Quiet,
Reserved;
Sunday School Teacher,
Piano Player,
and Church Secretary;
Cat-Eye Glasses,
Pearl Necklace,
Pencil skirt,
Pointed-toe high heels
And Black Silk Stockings
With Seams up the back
Straight as an arrow
Like her

FELLOWSHIP SUNDAY

The Word
(God's Word that is)
The Bird
(Chicken that is)
Macaroni and Cheese
Potato Salad
Turnip Greens
Black-eyed Peas
Cornbread
Banana Pudding
Caramel Cake
Dressing
And did I say...
The Word?

VISITATION

How you been feeling?
Tol'able well
Fair to Middlin'
Comin' back this away
What should I say for the chuch report?
Oh..OK
Sister Jones is doing better
She hopes to be back in service
Next Sunday
And...
She sent her offering

HAT LADY

(Dedicated to the "Hat Ladies" in the church)

She struts her stuff,
Like a beautifully plumed bird.
Her head's adornment is outfitted
With feathers, fur, bows, and sparkly things.
It's tipped to the side
And dips seductively over one eye
As she peers out from under,
At her many admirers.
She knows she's looking good.
"Wear that hat girlfriend!"
I want to be a hat lady one day...
When I grow up.

BACK IN THE DAY

Back in the day
Cats were jivin'
Businesses were thrivin'
We were all vibin'
Back it in day
What happened?

◆ ❖ ◆

OLD SCHOOL (OLE SKOOL)

A certain walk
A certain talk
A certain sway
A certain way
A certain jive
A certain vibe
Old school

MISS NORTHSIDE

**(Dedicated to all of the past Miss Northsides
and Miss Northside Contestants)**

Our neighborhood beauty pageant
In the summertime
Was quite an event to see
In my 10th grade year, I decided,
The Miss Northside crown
Was waiting just for me
I bought a stunning bathing suit
And did my stomach crunches
Advice from everywhere on how to win
Came to me in bunches.
In my high heels, around the house,
I practiced my stallion walk;
And considering the question and answer period;
I practiced how I'd talk.
For my talent, I did a ballet dance,
And I must say very well;
In my eyesight, compared to me,
The competition paled.
Our big night finally came,
And we strolled around the pool;

The lights were bright
And the crowd was wild
But, I remained absolutely cool.
As it turned out,
I didn't get that winning Miss Northside cup
But, I considered it just as well,
I got 2nd runner up.

*1980 Miss Northside — Misty Douglas
1st Runnner Up — Carla Floyd
2nd Runner Up — Patricia Neely

DEBRO'S

One A.M.
Straight from the Elk's
Tired.
Hungry.
Ready to Eat
Sit on the stool
And peer at yourself in the glass
Fans turning
Grease burning
"What you need?"
"And what with that?
"Nehi Grape
Or Pepsi?"
Never disappointed
Two golden fried pan trout
On "light" bread
With fries
In a greasy paper sack
Mr Debro
Picasso of the pond
Serving up perfection

A.M. STRANGE LIBRARY

That little one room library on
North Green Street
Held a special place in our hearts.
It was our neighborhood place to go
For story hours, book reviews,
And exposure to the arts.
We'd sit at the little tables,
Or form circles on the floor;
We were ready for some grand adventure,
Each time we stepped in the door.
Mrs. Vaughn our wonderful librarian
Was so softspoken, kind and sweet;
With a warm smile and welcoming voice,
Each child there she would greet.
To many of us bookworms,
It's where we got our start;
And to my childhood love of reading,
It played a very intregral part.

BEAUTY SHOP

Reading
Relaxing
Relating
Enjoying pampering time
Walking away with a new look,
A new attitude and new NEWS
Our
Necessary
Sanctuary
Beauty shop

Remembering: Elsie's House of Beauty, Mildred's Beauty Shop, Zina's Beauty Shop, Annie's Hair It Is, and Delores' Beauty Nook

THE POOL HALL

The fellas gather
In a smoke filled room
Young and old
With juke box blaring
Winning
Losing
And "Trash Talking"
Sharing
Bonding
Late night
Til early morn
Goodbyes
Then home
To return again

THE CLUB

Dark
Crowded
Den of bodies
Chest to Chest
And Back to Back
Strobe lights turning,
Dance floor Hopping
And DJ Burning (it up)
Stolen Glances
Careless Whispers...
And Various Lies
"Can I get that number (them digits)?"
"Can I have this dance?"
"Can I get that chance?"
Last song
Slow Dance
Lights on
Then out

LANDMARKS

"Can you tell me how to get to..."
"Yeah, You know...
You go past the bridge and Lockridge Store,
Carver School, Ashby's, Debros, Mayhorns,
Tolbert's Funeral Home and The Tank
Turn by Lane Chapel and Brown's Cleaners
It's down from Vaughn's Motel and
Dr. Neely's office
Around from The RC Plant and Graysons
Across the Tracks
Over by The Packing House
You know..."
"Yeah, I know where that is...
I think."

BANKS

Dark as midnight
Sharp as a tack
Sporting that hat
That overcoat
Those sparkly rings
Thundering laugh
And mysterious smile
Whispering words of wisdom
"Hey, Little Neely...Come here!"
Street corner philosopher
E.F. Hutton of the Hood
Nice as can be...
But...Don't play!
Heart of Gold
But, don't cross him.

NEIGHBORHOOD GOSSIP
(Minding other folks' business)

"Why she put up wit' him?"
"Everybody know he ain't no count"
"Runnin' 'roun in them streets
"Stayin' out all time a night"
"He ain't sudyin' her"
"I know she know."
"Some folks just rather have a piece a man
Than no man at all"
"And jus' wearin' britches
Don't make you no man"
"He ain't worth two dead flies"
"I wouldn't have him!"
"And why she keep havin' all them babies?"
"They pretty though."
"Sho is!"

SOUL TRAIN

Saturday morning
Glued to the set
"It's on!!!!
"Sit down"
"Get out of the way"
Watching those moves
Memorizing those steps
The Penguin, The Pony,
The Four Corners
The Bus Stop
Checking out the Fashions
Afros, Hip Huggers, Bell Bottoms
And High Heeled stacks
Waiting for
Don Cornelius
The Scamble board
And the Soul Train Line
Amazed to see
Marvin, Al, Stevie, Gladys and
Aretha practically in the room;
The hippest Trip in the Nation
"You can bet your last money
It's gonna be a stone gas honey"
Until next week...
Wishing you Love, Peace...
and SOOOUUULLL!!!

DOUBLE DUTCH

Cords flying
Overlapping
In and Out
Over and Under
Up and Around
Licking at the ground
And kicking up (much) dust
"Swish Swish"
Watching, Watching
Rocking , Rocking
Back and Forth
Waiting, Waiting
"Run In!"
"Now!"

SPADES

"Who?"

"You?"

"Beat us?"

Please!!!!

"Y'all don't know nothin"

"bout playin' no Spades!"

"O.K...Just to shet y'all up..."

"Shuffle !"

"Cut!"

"Deal !"

"Bid"

"Play!"

"What you waitin' on?"

"You scared"

"Ain't no talkin' cross the board!"

"BAM'

"Take that"

"Yeah I'm cutting!"

"Now what??!!"

"Ten hand"

"You set!"

"NEXT!!!"

CAKE WALK

Church basement
Music playing
Chalk outline
Around the room
"Take a chance
It's for a good cause."
7up cake
Sock it to me Cake
Sour Crème Pound,
Caramel And Coconut
Walk...
Walk...
Slowly...
Carefully...
Pull my number
Please
"What?"
"Man!"
Another Dollar.

GOING TO TOWN

Making the Rounds
And Stopping in
Or Passing by
Ben Franklin
TKE
Kuhn's
Kent's
Kermit's Bakery
Pryor's
McGaugh's
Reed's
Westbrook's
Black's
Two Sisters
And of course, The Corner Shoe Store
We'd always make a day of it
Going to town.

MY CHILDHOOD ROOM (Pretty in Pink)

Pink Floral Curtains
Matching Spread
And Canopy
With lots of Ruffles
Pink Rocking chair
Pink "Princess" phone
And Pink walls
Of course
So pretty in pink
And so fitting
For a future AKA,
I think
"Keep the light on,
Please."

GETTING IN TROUBLE
(What Our Parents Would Always Say)

"Didn't I tell you?
"How many times do I have to tell you?"
"So, you think you grown, now?"
"Mary?"
"I don't care what Mary does...
I'm not Mary's mother."
"So, if Mary go jump off a bridge,
You gonna go jump off a bridge, too?"
"You live in my house, you go by my rules."
"God don't like ugly."
Don't you know...
"A hard head makes a soft behind."
(Long pause)
"Just wait til your father gets home."
(Dead silence)
Uhh ohh!!!

4TH OF JULY

Flags Waving
Fireworks Popping
Family reunion picnics
And a new outfit
Barbecue, Baked beans
Fried chicken, Cole Slaw
Watermelon,
Homemade Ice cream
And did I say...
A new outfit?

MAKING (Homemade) ICECREAM

Get out the churn
And fill the bucket
With the ice
And the salt
Next,
Add the cream
And the sugar
And vanilla
Then crank, crank, crank
And wait wait wait
For the most delightful
Confection

◆ ❖ ◆

UNDERSTOOD

Growing Up...
We all knew
The Store
The Corner
The Shortcut
The Hiding Place
The Candy lady
and...
The Rules

THE DEBUTANTE COUTILLON

This function that I speak of,
Was called our "coming out;"
To introduce us to "society,"
And all the people of clout.
We wore beautiful, white flowing gowns,
All pristine, pert and prim;
With ruffles, bows and appliques,
From our shoulders to our hems.
We did our practiced curtsies,
With handsome escorts by our sides;
We all were properly presented,
As our parents beamed with pride.
It's a long standing tradition.
One continued year after year;
It's a once in a lifetime experience,
That each girl will always hold dear.

HOODOO LADY

My mama and daddy told me,
About a lady in their town
To whom folks would travel great distances,
nd come from all around.
What made these people come so far?
What did they come to hear?
Perhaps, many came out of sheer desperation,
And many others motivated by fear.
"Wear this trinket around your neck."
"Sprinkle this around your door"
"Put this pouch under your pillow"
"Plant this soundly under the floor."
She'd make her own medicines,
And concoct all kinds of potions;
For some ailment that you might have
There'd be funny smelling lotions.
There was a room in the back of her house,
Where no one could enter in;
It was her secret sanctuary,
Where her craft, there she would tend.
During the week she'd walk about ,
Looking frightfully tattered and torn;
But, on Saturdays she'd parade to town,
In the most extravagant garments worn.
She never married and had no kids,
But clients provided her life with honey;
For in her room, when she died,
Was a huge trunk full of money.

TUPELO SPIRIT (Tupelo, MS)

Heartily embracing history and heritage,
Past and Present
Forging faithfully forward
And celebrating a rockin', rollin' native son;
Inviting all to enjoy
Southern Hospitality at its finest
In the Mississippi Hills;
Always Hopeful,
Always Helpful,
The Tupelo Spirit shines bright.

TUPELO

The small town where I am from,
Get's its name from the Tupelo Gum.
No matter wher in the world,
That I might roam:
This is the palce that I call home.
Though I've been northeast for my education,
I've stayed fiercely Southern
In dedication.
In Memphis I lived for many years,
By my own election,
And even still, there was that
Tupelo connection.
At Elvis' Graceland,
Fans come to mourn;
But it's Tupelo, Mississippi,
Where I was born.
Tupelo is know as the All-American City
If you've never enjoyed it
That's quite a pity.
It's so warm, so hospitable and so neat,
Everything about it to me is so sweet.
I love the trees, the flowers and the birds,
I can't really describe all its beauty in words.

56

Though many places in my life
Have played a significant part;
It's Tupelo, Mississippi, y'all,
That still has all my heart.

*Previously published in <u>Reflections of a Mississippi
Magnolia-A Life in Poems</u>

THE BIRTHPLACE

Would anyone have suspected
The stories that these walls held
Of a mother working fingers to the bone
And a father who was jailed?
All the secrets that lived inside,
The world would not have known;
If the young man with the old guitar
Had not ascended to his throne.
Would anyone have wanted to know
About the family from "across the tracks,"
Who could hardly keep food on the table
Or clothing on their backs?
Would anyone have even cared,
About the heartaches, pain and scorn
If this tiny frame house hadn't found acclaim
As the place where "The King" was born?

THE KING (Elvis A. Presley)
(born: Jan 8,1935, Tupelo, MS)

From poor and meager beginnings,
A young man began to sing;
From the small town of Tupelo,
A voice began to ring.
As surely as it's been said,
A man's gifts make a way for him;
This humble diamond
In the rough,
Became a sparkling gem.
Velvet melodies and
Explosive rock,
Were the gifts he'd bring;
The world responded
With resounding praise,
And pronounced this man
"The King."

REED'S DEPT. STORE
(Established 1905)

Reed's Dept. store in Tupelo,
Is the oldest in the town;
It was the place, as a child,
Where all our clothing needs were found.
Each year, in the fall, with my mom,
Before the start of school;
We'd go to Reed's for school attire.
This was just the rule.
When it was time for a winter coat,
It was off to Reed's we'd go;
So I'd be prepared for chilly days,
Or maybe even snow.
Reed's is where we'd always get,
Our uniforms for scouts;
If we needed a new cap or sash,
Reed's would have it, without a doubt.
Over the years, it stayed the same,
If we had special needs;
For fancy occasions or big events,
We'd always go to Reed's.

KUDZU LOVE

My love for you
Is like the kudzu,
That surrounds us
In this place;
Changing
the landscape
Of my life,
It is
Unyielding,
Unrelenting,
And cannot
Be contained.

PERFECT

If there has ever been a more perfect day,
I can't remember it;
And if I have ever loved you more,
I certainly cannot recall;
Everything is right with the world
(Or at least in my world)
And I want it,
you...us...this
To last...
Forever.

HOME

Like a bird in a feathered nest,
Or a rabbit in it's burrow
Your embraces keep me safe and
comfort me
Your smile warms me,
Your kisses engulf me,
And your voice lulls me to sleep.
I cannot tell the particular thing
That makes me know that you are
the only one for me
And with you is where I always want to be
All I know is
Everything about you
Says
HOME

TELL ME AGAIN

Tell me again how you love me,
Tell me again how you care;
Tell me again how no one else,
Can ever have what we share.
Tell me how you love me,
Tell me how you long;
Tell me how we're so right,
Without the least thing wrong.
Tell me you'll love me forever,
Tell me we'll always be;
Tell me again and again and again
How perfect we are
You and me.

EVERYTHING

I want to make you happy
I want to make you smile
I want to be the one
That you can count on
To go the extra mile
I want to be your lover
I want to be your friend
I want to be the one for you
Until the very end
I want to be your Everything
The one to help you soar
I want for you to drink me in
And never thrist for more

TOGETHER (Again)

Somewhere along our journey
We made a choice to part
Possibly we thought that another
Was meant to have our hearts
We tried again with others
A variety we did meet
But, no matter what,
We always found
The honey not as sweet
Days went by and seasons changed
Months turned into years
A longing ache and empty space
Would sometimes bring the tears
Somehow, with fates direction,
Our paths merged once again
And from that day, forever more
We vowed our love to tend
In all of this gigantic world
We found no one who could
Fulfil our needs and wants in every way
Like each other would
Now, we can't imagine life
Without the other there
And we cherish each precious moment
That we are blessed to share

THE SOFTER SIDE OF LIFE

You are an old fashioned man
I'm an old fashioned girl
We want to live
In an old-fashioned world
We want the softer side of life
Without the harsh cold edge
Where man and woman intertwine
Without some competitive wedge
We look for easy, quiet times
In all the things we do;
With jazzy tunes and full lit moons
And hectic moments few.
We like a slower, measured pace,
No Rushing here and there;
We like to stop and smell the roses
And take the upmost care
We like the little niceties
That others push aside
We like the little curtisies
And from them do not hide
We notice all the little things
As we go along our way
A dazzling sun
A crisp white sheet
A blade of glass beneath our feet
A knowing glance
A sparkling smile
Are things that we hold dear
And we both feel certain
That things are better
When the other one is near.

MY FAVORITE RESTAURANT

I have a favorite restaurant
Where the food is exactly right
It never fails to always be
Exactly what I like
You can tell that it's prepared
With tender, loving care
And there's no better service to be found
Almost anywhere
It's real homecooking
It's real soul food
There's ambiance lighting
And just the right mood
This restaurant is in my house
My dining room's the spot
And there's my man,
My own gourmet cook
Stirring in the pot

THE EYES HAVE IT

We have our own language
That we speak
Without words.
Our eyes meet across the room
You say
"Are you O,K.?"
I say...
Yes, I'm fine."
You say...
"You need anything?"
I say...
"No, but thanks for asking."
You say...
"You want to go home?"
I say...
"Yes,
Let's."

THE TRUCK

Riding along
Feet on the dash
Sun in my face
And wind through my hair
It's just where I want to be
Right beside him
In his truck

◆ ❖ ◆

IT

You could never stop me,
From loving you the way I do;
There is No one or No thing that can;
I cannot even stop my self,
Even though, I've tried;
I will always love you.
That's just the way it is.
You're IT...for me.

ABERRATION

When I say to my man
"You're so distant"
"You seem so detached"
"I don't feel like you're hearing me"
"I don't feel like you care"
He says
"Be serious
"That could never be
"You're just seeing a ghost
"What?"
"Seeing a ghost
"You're just imagining things."
"Letting your mind play tricks on you."
"Seeing something that's not there"
"Seeing a ghost"
"Oh..."
"OK."

THE GAME OF LOVE

I know that my man has a mistress,
She is that game of golf;
He desires every inch of her presence,
And breathes her in every breath.
He loves visiting her green gardens,
And he knows every crevice and hole
He thinks that she's a magnificent creature
And to him she never grows old
In springtime, I become a golf "widow"
And secretly consider divorce
But, because I know how I love that man
I just chalk it up par for the course.

CHILD'S PLAY or The Love Game?

**Red Rover Red Rover send that one right
over
Mother may I?
My Mama told me to pick...this...One
(But) Simon says...
You're it!
Red Light Green Light
Stop (The madness)!**

(NOT) CINDERELLA

I must admit...
I used to believe
In fairytales...
And dreams come true.
I was supposed to be the princess
And you my prince charming.
We were supposed to live happily ever after
And all of that...
Just like in the storybooks.
But, before we could turn all the pages...
Together,
You said:
"The End"

BURNED

Like a moth to a flame,
I was drawn to your brilliant light
I got too close
And was burned

HEARTBREAK (This Too, Shall Pass)

Numb,
Empty,
Hoping,
Groping,
Searching,
Crying,
Dying...
Then, moving on

QUESTIONS

Who is this one
Who has taken my place
In your life,
In your heart
And your mind?
What does she do for you
That I didn't do
Or couldn't do
Or wouldn't do
If you asked?
Where was I
When all of this happened?
And, why didn't I see?
I'm just asking.

SEASONS OF LOVE

It has been winter between us
For too long
Cold, barren,
Dorment and Unyielding.
I shiver
Seeking warmth.
It has been winter between us
For too long
Do you even remember the spring?

INVISIBLE

You used to say
Don't you know I see you?
I see everything about you
And I felt that you did
Now, you look straight through me,
Around me and past me
Like I'm not even in the room
You don't notice me at all
It's like...
I'm invisible
I don't think that's what they meant
When they said
Love is blind

LOVE HURTS (Battle Wounds)

I'm finding that
This "love thing"
Can be a cold nasty business
Is that why they say
All is fair in love and war?
Why did I think that
I could come out
Unscathed?
No such luck
I've been wounded.

DISCONNECT

I'm trying to get through to you
I'm talking but you are not hearing
I'm sending but you're not receiving
There seems to be a lot of static
And some outside interference
Is something or someone else intercepting?
Are our batteries low?
Do we need to recharge?
Or am I just a dropped call?
Maybe, I need to try this again.
Can you hear me now?

WHO I BE?

Who I Be?
I Be Me.
But, there's much more to me,
Than the me you see.
I can be sunlight and laughter
Or storm clouds and rain;
I might cry when I'm happy
Or even laugh when in pain.
I am sometimes the anchor
And sometimest the sail
I'm often successful,
But sometimes I fail.
Sometimes, I'm exactly
What you think, hope, want
Or expect me to be
But most importantly,
I Be Me.

FLAVOR

I've got flavor.
Like jazz music...
Which they say is
A perfect blend
Of musical styles
That makes that smooth
Intoxicating , soulful sound
And like a delicious gumbo
Which takes lots of
Relatively ordinary ingredients
Mixed together to make
An extra ordinary dish
I've got flavor.
It takes a perfect combination
Of a little bit of this
And a little bit of that
A pinch of this
And a pinch of that
Put together
In just the right way
To REALLY have flavor.
I've got flavor.

MY POEMS

It's a wonderful thing,
That somehow through poems
You can know what I known
And go where I've gone.
It's amazing
That through
Just a few simple words
You can see what I've seen
And hear what I've heard.
There's such a joy in sharing,
Even in part;
So much of my thinking,
And even more of my heart.

◆ ❖ ◆

ENOUGH

I don't need some literary prize
Or glory
Or fame
For what I write
If I write what I feel
And feel what I write
And like it
Then you read it
And tell me you like it, too
I think to myself,
That's enough.

SISTAH FRIENDS

My sistah friends,
Our lives are all
Intertwined,
Intermingled,
Interlocked;
Absolutely,
Concretely,
Completely,
Somehow.
We are a part of the constant ebb and flow
Of the universe and the circle of life.
It is proclaimed
"Enter these portals and learn
Depart and give to others."
"Enter what portals?" we say.
"Give what to others?" we ask.
We enter the portals of Life, of Love, of
Marriage, Divorce,
Heartbreak, Hardship, Heartaches.
We learn lessons,
Sometimes, very hard lessons.
We must give from those lessons learned
Pour out the elixers
From the wellsprings, the pitchers of
Knowledge and wisdom
For others to drink

To be filled, refreshed, renewed and revived.
It is our duty to God, to our forefathers,
To others and to ourselves.
It is our duty to give back, to share,
To assist, to contribute.
As those who have gone on before us,
Who helped us to to navigate
The winding paths,
We must teach, inspire, encourage,
Help and heal.
Like it has been done for each of us
Like it has been given to each of us
We must do the same.
Swaying back and forth on those
Old wooden benches
In that old country church
Our mothers had us in mind
Had our futures in mind
Had this future in mind
As they sang
To us, about us, for us
My Sistah friends
The Circle of Friends
May The Circle Be Unbroken
May The Circle Be Unbroken
By and By Lord
By and By.

MY PEOPLE

What has happened to my people,
To the soul and the pulse that we share?
Where are the signs we're cohesive,
Or evidence that most even care?
What are the things that we value,
The manner of life we hold dear?
Where is the pulling together,
And letting go of all fear?
Do we still seek to make our world better
And unite together as one?
Or is each one out for his lonesome,
With essentially nothing getting done?
It saddens my heart to see how we've gone,
From a people who once excellence sought;
To the way we exist and the state of affairs,
Where a proud history seems all gone for
nought.

WE LIKE TO READ...TOO
(In memory of the W.A. Zuber Reading Club)

Yes, we like to party and dance and sing
And shout
But, we like to read, too.
We might have been someone's maid or nanny
Or cook or back door guest
But, we like to read, too.
We might have been dead tired from
Standing over a hot stove all day
(our own or someone else's)
But, we like to read, too
Our parents might have only had
A 6th grade education
Or sharecropped on some farmer's land
But, we like to read, too.
We like to explore all those places,
Feel all those feelings,
Dream all those dreams
And learn all those things
That books allow
And as unbelievable as it might seem,
To some folks, to many folks, to other folks
Or to those folks
We, Like to Read, too.

THE FAMILY TREE

We are a glorious tree
With beautiful branches outstretched,
Reaching toward the heavens;
Offering our various gifts
And fruits of our labor.
We share common roots,
That run deep in ancestral soil;
Nurtured by
Common purpose,
Faith, heritage and hope.
We hear the whispers and shouts
Of those gone before.
We hear the voices
Of that great cloud of witnesses,
Ever urging, prodding, coaxing ;
Giving meaning to our race,
Shedding light on our pathways
We carry a certain knowledge
Deep within us
Embedded within our very bones
And marrow;
Encoded in the blood,
That runs between us
Among us and through us;

Carrying a sacred message
Imparted across generations.
We stand united,
Singing praises
To the One
Who made us,
Gathered us,
And bound us
Into a
Strong,
Proud,
Distinctive
Family Tree

ONE

Our lives are all
Intertwined,
Intermingled,
Interlocked,
Absolutely,
Completely,
Somehow.
As in the marriage ceremony
When the minister explains the rings
As symbols,
As circles
Representing a continuum
Representing the unending
So are we
You and me.
I am in you
And you are in me;
We are connected,
Somehow.
We have been pronounced one
By the Universe,
By common experiences,
Common bloodlines,

Shared histories, shared heritages, shared hopes
A part of the constant ebb and flow
Of the Universe
Part of the circle of life.
Like the individual colorful, varied pieces
Of a quilter's pattern
Woven intricately together...
Seamlessly
To make one beautiful whole
Each piece important...
In the completeness
So are we...a magnificent collage
Of hands, faces, bodies,
Spirits, hearts and minds,
With voices blending together
To make one harmonious symphony of sound.
Like the church, being many members
Yet, one body...
So are we...
One organism
One being
From one common life source
Experiencing the same that life offers to all
Birth, death, heartache, heartbreak
Love, Loss
Laughter and Tears

We are more alike than different
More the same than unique..
Although...we are unique.
Across generations, colorlines, territories,
tribes,regions, religions
Ideologies, and beliefs
We remain the one..
Human Race.
Let us then revel in
And not rebel against
Our oneness
Fight for and not against
Our Oneness
Let us
Enjoy,
Embrace and
Celebrate,
Our Oneness
For, we are...surely
One.

(Origianlly written for the Oren Dunn City Museum Unity
Jubilee -Tupelo, MS)

CONSOLATION

If you're always thinking the sky is falling,
And are a Henny Penny like the old version of me;
Somebody needs to let you know,
"What will be, will be".
No matter how dark the path may look,
Or even how scary the way;
Be reminded constantly,
Tomorrow's a brand new day.
Though many things may go awry,
Regardless of all the rest;
The sun will most assuredly rise in the east,
And most definitely set in the west.
The sun'll come out tomorrow,
I know, it most certainly will;
You can't get caught up in worry,
Just continue to climb up that hill.
Keep your wits about you,
And negative thoughts at bay;
Maintain a positive attitude,
And it certainly wouldn't hurt to pray.
There's light at the end of the tunnel,
And a rainbow at the end of the storm;
But, somehow, we seem to reason,
That to worry is simply the norm.

My mantra is, "It's not that serious",
It really never is;
They say don't sweat the small stuff,
But, it's all small through eyes like HIS.
When you've done all that YOU can do,
You've done ALL that you can do;
Somehow, you must remember,
It's simply not up to you.
I know you've heard the song that says
The battle is not yours;
You must somehow realize,
It's to the Lord deferred.
God says in His word not to worry,
For who by worrying can possibly add
One cubit to his stature
Or even one single hair to his head.
It's really just that simple,
You do what you can do;
Then give all else to the Lord,
And he'll take care of you.

FEAR(LESS)

Fear not my little ones, he says
Don't worry and don't fret
I will supply your every need
And make sure each one is met.
David testified that from young to old,
He was protected, clothed and fed
And never had seen the righteous forsaken
Or his seed ever begging bread.
Paul proclaimed that no matter the trial
One's sure belief should be
That I can do and edure all things
Through Christ who strengthens me
Daniel, even, in the lion's den
Told anyone who had an ear.
That his God was able to deliver him
And in this he had no fear.
All throughout God's holy writ
We are assured most infatically
As children in his kingdom
He will care for you and me
Its clear that we should always trust
And never have need for fear
For He will guard, protect and shield us
Through his providential care

THE ROCK (of Ages)

When troubles and trails come your way,
And all your hope seems pale;
The comfort found in trusting God
Is one that never fails.
He's the first and final answer
In every conflict, and every woe
He is the sure and solid rock,
The one that we all should know
When fear threatens to overtake our lives
And put us in a bind
God is the number one defense
To clear and ease the mind
Through God's strength we can overcome,
Any giant enemy or foe;
He is the weapon of choice
In this fight called life
If victory we are to know.

WONDERING

Have you ever noticed how delicate
Are the wings of a dragonfly?
Then why are we afraid?

IF MISSISSIPPI'S IN YOU

If Mississippi's in you,
It'll always be that way;
It matters not how far you go,
Or how long you stay.
If Mississippi's in you,
It always plays a part;
In how you live and move and breathe,
And in every notion of the heart.
If Mississippi's in you,
It's in you through and through;
It's in in who you are and how you be,
And it's in everything you do.
If Mississippi's in you,
There is some special glow;
A different something down inside,
That all the home folks know.
If Mississippi's in you,
It'll always be that way,
From the time you enter in the world,
Till in the grave you lay.
Every true Mississippian,
Can surely have it said;
I'm Mississippi born,
I'm Mississippi bred,
And when I die,
I'll be Mississippi dead.

* Previously published in <u>Reflections of a Mississippi</u>
<u>Magnolia-A Life in Poems</u>

INTERESTING MISSISSIPPI TRIVIA:

▶ The magnolia tree is Mississippi's state tree and the magnolia is the state flower..thus the nickname, "The Magnolia State."

▶ Mississippi women are often referred to as Mississippi Magnolias.

▶ In 1929, chemist Harry A. Cole of Jackson, Mississippi invented Pine-Sol.

▶ Tennessee Williams, the Pulitzer Prize winning playwright who wrote such plays as "A Street Car Named Desire," "Cat on a Hot Tin Roof" and "The Glass Menagerie," was actually born in Columbus, Mississippi. He changed his name in 1939 to Tennessee, which is the state of his father's birth.

▶ Jim Henson, creator of The Muppets and other beloved Sesame Street characters was born in Columbus, MS.

▶ Blues music sprouted from the Mississippi's Delta and hill country. B.B. King, world renowned blues singer/guitatist, was born in Itta Bena, Mississippi.

▶ Oprah Winfrey was born in Kosciusko, Mississippi.

▶ Naomi Sims, black supermodel of the 70's and 80's, was born in Oxford, Mississippi.

▶ The first-ever heart transplant and the first-ever kidney transplant were performed by Mississippian Dr. James Hardy, a surgeon at Mississippi's University Medical Center.

▶ The 4-H Club, first known as the "Corn Club" was started in Holmes County, Mississippi in 1907.

▶ The first chapter of the PTA was formed in Mississippi in 1909.

▶ The world's first heavyweight championship fight took place in Mississippi City, Mississippi in 1882.

▶ Mississippi University for Women in Columbus was the first state college for women in the country, established in 1884.

▶ S.B. Sam Vick of Oakland, MS was the first and only baseball player to ever pinch hit for the baseball great Babe Ruth.

▶ Walter Payton of Columbia, MS was the first football player on a Wheaties box

▶ Joseph Biedenharn of Vicksburg, MS was the first person to bottle Coca-Cola in 1894.

▶ The first bottle of Dr. Tichener's Antiseptic was produced in Liberty, MS.

▶ Borden's condensed milk was first canned in Liberty, MS.

▶ Mississippi is the leading producer of farmed raised catfish in the U.S., accounting for 45-55 percent

▶ Mississippi was the first state in the nation to have a planned system of junior colleges.

Recommended Reading:

Reflections Of A Mississippi Magnolia —A Life in Poems
by Patricia Neely-Dorsey
ISBN: 978-0-979629 426, Paperback ◆ $ 15.00
Published 2008, by GrantHouse Publishers

PATRICIA NEELY-DORSEY
Reflections of a Mississippi Magnolia-A Life in Poems
" a celebration of the south and things southern"
"Meet Mississippi Through Poetry, Prose and The Written Word"
www.patricianeelydorsey.webs.com

"To understand the world, you must first understand a place like Mississippi"
—William Faulkner

CPSIA information can be obtained at www.ICGtesting.com
Printed in the USA
LVOW05s1309220114

370498LV00004B/792/P